PRAISE FOR

MY GOD

My Dear Lord

By
Allen Haberman

PublishAmerica
Baltimore

First printing

At the specific preference of the author, PublishAmerica allowed this work to remain exactly as the author intended, verbatim, without editorial input.

ISBN: 1-4241-7862-2
PUBLISHED BY PUBLISHAMERICA, LLLP
www.publishamerica.com
Baltimore

Printed in the United States of America

PRAISE FOR MY GOD

My Dear Lord

Oh Lord, My God—Jesus

Oh Lord, my God—Jesus,
Take me. Make me part of your vine.
Plant your word in the soil of my heart.
Make the roots grow.
The fibers binding tightly,
Strengthening me,
Holding together what was loose and weak.

Oh Lord, my God—Jesus,
Show me your ways. Make your word clear.
Grow blooms, of knowledge of you, in me.
Make the buds grow,
The blossoms revealing you.
Open my eyes.
The petals shining brightly even in deepest night.

Oh Lord, my God—Jesus,
Shape me. Form me to your will.
Break from me all that displeases you.
Make me let go.
The withered limbs removed,
Pruning me,
Taking away what is dead and hinders growth.

Oh Lord, my God—Jesus,
Use me. Make your vine show in me.
Set my branch more firmly on your trunk.
Make my faith grow.
The Word living within,
Feeding me,
Making of me what you intended from the start.

Crush Me, Lord

Crush me, Lord.
Destroy me.
All that was—your hands make new.

Purify me, Lord.
Cleanse me.
Set me apart—for your blessed use.

Mold me, Lord.
Shape me.
Make of me—a wholly holy vessel.

Temper me, Lord.
Strengthen me.
Shape me completely—to your perfect will.

Teach me, Lord.
Fill me.
Sate my soul—with your true word.

Overtake me, Lord.
Bless me.
Live in me—make me your temple.

Protect me, Lord.
Guard me.
Spread over me—your great unfailing wings.

Armor me, Lord.
Gird me.
Bind my faith—surrounded in your power.

Send me, Lord.
Use me.
Show through me—all your great love.

Without and with You

What am I without you?
I am formless—without feature.
I am lost—and void.
I am worthless—only dust.

What do I have without you?
All that I pursue—eludes me.
All that I hope—is vapor.
All that I have—is taken.

What is there without you?
Your hand—made the universe.
Your hand—stretched out time.
Your hand—formed all life.

With you, I am lifted up.
I am given form—and shaped.
I am found alive—without lack.
I am your creation—highly prized.

With you, I have your blessings.
All I pursue—is your will.
All I hope—is in you.
All I have—is your gift.

With you, there is all good things.
Your hand—made the universe.
Your hand—stretched out time.
Your hand—formed all life.

My Dear Lord

Lord, my dear Lord—in you I am kept safe.
I trust in you—Jesus.
All my grief is eased—by your loving hand.
All my weakness is overshadowed—by your great strength.
All my lack is removed—by your wonderful blessings.
All my fear is calmed—by all your glorious power.

Lord, my dear Lord—in you my path is sure.
I trust in you—Jesus.
Every adversary's heart is turned—by your loving hand.
Every obstacle is removed—by your great strength.
Every step is followed—by your wonderful blessings.
Every need is met—by all your glorious power.

Lord, my dear Lord—in you is all my hope.
I trust in you—Jesus.
All that is good—your hand formed.
All that has substance—your strength created.
All that I have—your blessings gave.
All that is yours—your power protects.

I am yours, Lord.
I trust in you—Jesus.

Holy Spirit

I long, for your Holy Spirit:
Your holy fire,
Your discerning flame.

Whose flames take only that which is dead
That burns only chaff.
Whose fire leaves only that which is pure
That which truly lives.
Your Holy Spirit that is reflected,
Only in perfected love.

I yearn, for your Holy Spirit:
The Great Comforter,
Your ever-present truth.

Who is sent only by your sacrifice;
Your life given for my sin.
Who gives guidance only to the believer;
Your word testified to within.
Your Holy Spirit that speaks
Only the Father's awesome will.

I ache, for your Holy Spirit:
Your overcoming power,
Your unfailing wisdom.

Your wisdom, opened within my heart;
My eyes, finally seeing.
Your power, released in my life,
Taking all my weakness.
The Holy Spirit that assures
Who gives me joy in adversity.

Father—send the Holy Spirit.
Jesus—send the Comforter.
Holy Spirit—come.

What I Need, Lord

You are my strength. In what way am I weak?
I am weak only—in my turning away from you.
When I rely only—on my own power:
What my own hand can do.
Your strength is what I need, Lord.

You heap upon me blessings. In what way am I poor?
I am poor only—in my turning away from you.
When I pursue only—the riches of the earth:
What my own hand can gain.
Your blessings are what I need, Lord.

You stand guard about me. In what should I fear?
I am fearful only—in my turning away from you.
When I stand alone—in my own willfulness:
What my own hand can defend.
Your Protection is what I need, Lord.

You guide me faultlessly. In what way am I lost?
I am lost only—in my turning away from you.
When I follow only—after my own path:
What my own eye can discern.
Your guidance is what I need, Lord.

You show me kindness upon kindness. In what should I despair?
I despair only—in my turning away from you.
When I refuse to see—that all is in your hand
That your heart is always toward me.
Your kindness is what I need, Lord.

You love me without bounds. In what way am I forsaken?
I am not forsaken. I have turned myself to you.
By your worthy sacrifice—paying for my sin,
I am cleansed in your holy blood.
Your love is what I need, Lord.

You Came After Me, Lord

You came after me, Lord.
You heard my plea—found me lost and led my way.
You guide me safely, Lord.
The path is narrow—and you know it.
I pursue you, Lord.
I've heard your word—found it good and thirst for more.
I am following after you, Lord.
I hear your voice—and I know it.

I yearn for you.
I long for your peace, your comfort—the loving heart of my God.
I hunger for you.
I long for your bounty, your blessing—the perfect will of my God.
I thirst for you.
I long for your touch, your presence—the indwelling spirit of my God.
I rest in you.
I trust in your rule, your power—the overwhelming might of my God.

Jesus, My Friend

Jesus, you are my friend,
My friend who is always there.
Every time I fall—you lift me up.
My every tear—you wipe away.
I love you now; you loved me first.

Jesus, you are my friend,
My friend who guides me true.
You led the way; I follow you.
You light the way; my path is clear.
I love you now; you loved me first.

Jesus, you are my friend,
My friend who gave your all
Your life lived true—by the Father's will.
You gave your life; you paid my price.
I love you now; you loved me first.

Jesus, you are my friend,
My friend above all friends.
All of your lashes—are my sins due.
All Your life's blood—shed to save me.
I love you now; you loved me first.

In You

Oh, my Lord—Jesus
I am not weak.
I am strong—in you.

I am not tired.
I am vigorous—in you.

I am not sad.
I have great joy—in you.

I am not in bondage.
My shackles are broken—in you.

I am not poor.
I have great treasure—in you.

I am not empty.
I am overflowing—in you.

I am not in darkness.
I am led by the light—in you.

I am not in fear.
I am assured—in you.

I am not in defeat.
I am an over-comer—in you.

I am not anything,
The world would have me be.
I am, as you would have me be;
I am your creation.

You are my God.
You are my King.
You have set me free.
And, I am free.

Oh, how free I am.
Oh, Lord—Jesus,
I am free—in you.

My Only Rest

Father, you were my only rest,
My only comfort—my peace.
The assurance I had in you:
The strength to overcome—to stand.
I knew you kept me safe—alive.

Father, I took upon myself,
What your might had done—your strength.
I gave to myself the glory.
The glory that was—your due.
I forgot your hand in—my life.

Father, where I had given you,
The glory, the praise—your due,
For the victories you gave me.
I took for prides sake—your might,
Called it my own to raise—my name.

Father, the more I would recall
Your awesome power—as mine.
The more fearful I would become.
I once stood with strength—certain.
Without you fear and doubt—took me.

Father, my mind and my heart
Could find no rest—no peace.
I thought back to what I once had:
To my God, my rest—my peace.
I had sinned against you—my Lord.

Father, you were always my strength:
My courage, my rock—my God.
It was you I could rely on.
How vain, how blinded—I was.
How weak I found myself—barren.

Father, I cast down all my pride.
I repent of all—my great sin.
With you my cares are taken away.
Dear Lord, you are my—only rest.
You are my only comfort—my peace.

Dying to Self

I have lived to myself: life without life,
Living in my sin, truly dead.
I have given only to myself: imprisoned in the world,
Living in my lusts, truly bound.
I have followed my own way: with no clear path,
Living in my ignorance, truly lost.
I have pursued the world's knowledge: knowledge devoid of truth,
Living in a lie, deceived.

The more I die to myself, the more I live:
Living in your will, truly alive.
The more I give myself to you, the freer I am:
Living in your will, truly free.
The more I follow your way, the clearer my path:
Living in your will, never lost.
The more I pursue your word, the greater my knowledge:
Living in your will, in truth.

The more I praise you—my Father. The happier I am.
The more I turn to you—my Lord. The more you turn to me.
The closer I get to you—Holy Spirit. The closer you get to me.
The happier I am in you—my God. The happier you are in me.
More and more
More and more
More and more, Lord
I want you—more and more, my God

I Thank You So

I thank you so, dear Lord—Jesus,
For all you have done.
You thought of me, and made me.
You gave me life—for your pleasure.
You have stood—in my place.
You paid a price—only you could pay.
You gave your perfect life—as a gift.
You have forgiven—my every sin.
You have saved me—time and again.
You have given me—strength in my weakness.
You have blessed me—for your own sake.
For no reason—I can discern.

I have accepted your gift—I glory in it.
I am yours.
All my sins—have been washed away.
I am new—at your hand.
Make of me—all that is in your will, for me to be.

The Day of Christmas

On this the day of Christmas,
We give gifts to those we love.
We do this in remembrance of the greatest gift ever given:

Of a little child born to a virgin,
The son of the one true God,
Who was and is God,
The Lord Jesus,
The Christ.

He gave his life for those he loves:
The world,
You and me, and all those who accept his gift.
The gates of heaven are open before us.
We are accepted before God's throne.
For us, we go from life to life more abundant.

Praise the Father, who sent his son.
Praise Jesus, who opened the way.
Praise the Holy Spirit, who is ever with us.
Praise God, always.

You Are the Lord God

You are the Lord God:
One of the three who are one,
The one true God—in heaven,
You are that you are,
The Great I Am.

The creator of all things:
Time had its start at your hand;
You spoke,
And all that is came into being,
Directed by your word.

I was a fallen child of Adam:
Born into sin,
A mere gathering of dust,
A creation of your hand,
Nothing—but for you.

Blind to all your creation:
Time bound me to but a few years;
To live then back to dust,
Destined for hell,
Left with no hope—alone.

Lord, you had mercy on your creation:
Adams children.
Jesus, you left your throne in heaven,
Took up the mantle of a man on earth,
Lived a life—fully in the Fathers will.

Unmarred by sin—a perfect offering,
Led to the slaughter—you willingly died.
Your life's blood—shed—for all sin for all time.
Save the sin of refusing your gift.
You rose again after three days; death's hold is broken.

I have accepted your gift—my Savior.
Jesus, Your holy blood covers me.
The life is in the blood.
Your life covers me.
The life, only you could live.
I am perfect before the Father because, your life covers me.

How wonderful it is to live in your mercy and your grace:
To be blessed at your hand,
To serve you and to know your love,
To be saved out of the world,
Accepting your gift, of joyous never-ending life spent with you.

Express Your Love Before the Lord

Express your love before the Lord.
Make plain your love for him.

Sing—sing of the love he has for you.
Sing—of he, who held nothing back.
Sing—of the Father, who gave his only son.
Sing—of the Lord, who gave up his throne.
Sing—oh, sing and sing before God.

Clap—for the son, born to a virgin.
Clap—for the boy, the angels proclaimed.
Clap—for the boy, who was called out of Egypt.
Clap—for the boy, who taught the teachers.
Clap—oh, clap and clap before God.

Jump—for the man, who is the pure spotless Lamb.
Jump—for the man, whose name is Jesus, who is Lord.
Jump—for Jesus, who taught and healed the world.
Jump—for Jesus, who was wounded and died to save us.
Jump—oh, jump and jump before God.

Dance—for he rose again. His grave is empty. We are set free.
Dance—for he was lifted up, and sits beside the Father.
Dance—for Jesus, the risen King of Kings.
Dance—for the Father, who loves us without bound.
Dance—oh, dance and dance before God.

Turned to You

Father, keep me—turned to you:
To your will,
To follow the path—you have for me,
To release—my will,
To hold to you—in all my ways.

Father, I have followed—worldly ways.
All are empty.

Every goal I've pursued,
Each plan I've made,
Separate from you,
I lay down—I release.

All that I have hoped for,
No matter how great,
Is less—is nothing
Compared to the plans—you have for me.

In that—I have prospered.
You would have given me—true treasure.
In that—I have loved.
You would have shown me—true love.
In that—I had strength.
You would have born—all my weakness.
In that—I was wise.
You would have given me—true wisdom.

In every way—I thought I was strong.
You are stronger. You are unfailing.
I am weak. I am nothing before you.
Still—you love me. You jealously pursued me.
You gave everything—to save me.
Now, I am turned to you. I love you, Father.
You have always—loved me.

I will follow you. I will follow your ways.
Father—you made me. You know me.
You created me—with a purpose.
Set me—to your purpose.
In this—I will be happy.
I will be satisfied.
In your will—I will be fulfilled.

Lord, I Look to You

Lord, I look to you.
You are my teacher,
My friend—my healer.
You are my provider,
My rescuer—my redeemer.
You are my true counsel,
My creator—my everything.

Lord, all is in your hand.
What in all the earth—is not yours to give
To do with—as you will?
What in all the universe—is not created by your Word
That is not subject—to your command?

The deepest pit in hell to your throne in heaven
All is yours.

Satan and all who fell with him—every demon:
Full of pride—their hearts turned from you,
With dark hard hearts—and full of rage,
Their every thought—is of destruction.
Lord, you command—and they obey.

The whole host of heaven—every angel, saint, and living creature:
Filled with love for you—their hearts exultant in your rule,
With giving willing hearts—and filled with adoration,
Their every thought—is for good—your will.
Lord, you command—and they obey.

I am but a man—a passing breath, soon to sleep; saved by you.
Filled with thanksgiving—my heart is turned to you.
With a softened loving heart—full of gladness,
My every thought—is of praise for you.
Lord, you command—and I obey.

Lord, you rule over all.
Yet, your heart and your attention—are turned to me.
You have shown me love. You have blessed me.
You have taught me—given me knowledge.
You have taken me—from a low place, and raised me up.
You have forgiven me—and taken me as your own.

I look to you—Jesus. I wait on you.
You are, my Lord—my King—my God.

Lord, Train Me

Lord, train me.
Ready me for battle.
Train me, in how to wear your armor.
Train me, in the use of your shield.
Train me, in the wielding of your sword—your word.

Lord, set me to sparring.
Build my skills.
Increase my understanding.
Make of me a warrior in your service.

Set my feet firmly in your peace,
The peace that is beyond all comprehension,
So that I will not be shaken.
My heart my every thought bound in Christ, who is Jesus.

Wrap about me the belt of your truth,
The truth that is revealed in your word,
So that I will stand against every deceit.
No lie will stand against your word—your truth.

Place upon me the breastplate of your righteousness.
The righteousness given for belief in Christ Jesus,
So that I will keep to your will—that only you will show through me.
It is your righteousness, Lord, that covers me.

Set upon my head the helmet of salvation,
The salvation you have given me. That you have given the world,
So that my focus is on the good news of Jesus the Christ:
The saving of souls through the Lords sacrifice at the cross.

On my one arm set the shield of faith,
The faith I have in you, Lord,
So that every attack of the enemy is deflected.
Against this shield he cannot prevail,
For you are faithful and true.

In the hand of my other arm place the sword of your Spirit,
Your word—oh, God;
So that both edges of the blade of your word do their work.
Lay bare the heart. Lay bare the mind.
Separate what is false from what is true.

Lord, prepared by your hand,
In the day of battle,
I will don the whole armor of God.
I will stand and glory at your victories.

Your Correction

Lord, how good you are.
Though I stray—I will always turn to you.
You are always loving—in your correction.
You guide me.
You take me back—to the right path:
Away from the lure—of false things,
Away—from harm
Away—from death.
Your correction—leads me down the path of truth:
Toward—what is good,
Toward—what is life,
Toward—the dwelling place of love,
Toward you—Lord Jesus.

Lord—I Am Yours

Lord—I am yours.
In what way am I not?
Before the beginning,
In your thoughts, you conceived me.
With your wisdom and your skill you made me.
You Lord—placed me in my mother's womb.
To be born into the world you made.

All the days of my life I have lived
Eating your food, drinking your water,
Breathing your air, walking on your earth.

Not only have you made me and provide for me,
You paid for me and redeemed my every debt.
Not with gold, not with Silver, with something of true value,
Lord—Jesus, you sold your life for mine.
You laid it down as a gift.

With your gift, I am yours.
Without it, I am lost.
I receive it. I accept it.
Lord,—I am yours.

Lord, I Have Strayed

Lord, I have strayed.
I have followed after a strange path.
I am lost.
I call out to you.

It's not you who left me, Lord.
I left you.
I saw a flower that looked sweet.
It was a bitter weed.

You are the good shepherd.
Your ears are keen for the cries of your flock.
You hear me though I am far from you.
You come after me.
You will bring me again to good pasture.

No matter how far I fall.
You will come down and get me.
No matter how high I climb.
It's not too high for you.
No matter how far I stray from you, Lord.
You will find me.

When death and destruction seem near,
When I cry out to you, Lord;
When I say, "Save me, Lord;"
When I say, "I need you, Lord;"
You will not tarry.
Nothing will stand in your way.

Your life you have not held back to save me.
Though you were deeply wounded, you pursue me,
With a heavy burden, you did not stop to get to me,
All of your precious blood spilt to rescue me.
You have given everything to gather me to you.

Prayer

Father, not only are you able—it is your will
to release your blessings, your healing power,
your strength, and your protection on your people.

Father, you sent my Lord Jesus, to gather me up to you.
You sent your son to be broken so that I could be healed.
My God, you spilled out your life to save my life.

Yet,
How sad it is, Father, that so often I call to you
But, my faith only sees your might:
Your unmatched power, that you are able.

How sad it is, Father, that so often my prayers—lack faith.
They do not see to your heart:
To your love, the good that is your will.

How good it will be, Father, on the day I call to you,
And my faith has grown always seeing beyond your might:
Your boundless all encompassing power, that you are able.

How good it will be, Father, on the day my prayers are as they should be
Full of faith, always seeing to your heart,
To your love, to your blessed holy will,
That you desire to bless us with all your promises.

How glad I'll be, Father, when my faith is fully in you.
To not only know, but to trust that your will is for my good,
For the good of all who serve you,
Even that the whole world would turn to you, to know you.

How glad I will be, Father, when your will
Can more fully be done in my life.
The fullness of your love poured out on me.
Finally, the servant you want me to be.

Only in You

It is only in you, that I am truly strong.
Nothing of me—endures.
Nothing of me—overcomes.
It is you, my God. You are the strength over all my weakness: your power
Through Jesus.

It is only in you, that I have real peace.
Nothing of me—is calm.
Nothing of me—wants to wait.
It is you, my God. You are the peace that surrounds me: your Spirit
Through Christ.

It is only in you, that I know real love.
Nothing of me—is giving.
Nothing of me—thinks of another.
It is you, my God. You are the love that lives within me: your presence
Through the Lord.

It is only in you, that I have true wisdom.
Nothing of me—knows truth.
Nothing of me—seeks understanding.
It is you, my God. You are my true consul: the fount of all true knowledge,
Of all true wisdom; your mind
Through your Word.

You are—my strength, and I know it.
You are—my peace, and I know it.
You are—my love, and I know it.
You are—my wisdom, and I know it.
You are—my everything, and I know it.

No Matter

Father,
No matter, if I feel your spirit upon me
Or, if he seems far from me.
I will raise my hands to you.
I will raise my voice and sing.
I will move my feet and dance.
I will jump and show my love for you.

Father, though there are times I don't feel your presence.
I know you are there.
You are with me.
Your thoughts are toward me.
You are my Father, and you love me.
This is what your Word says, and your Word is true.

So,
I will raise my hands to you.
I will raise my voice and sing.
I will move my feet and dance.
I will jump and show my love for you.

My Father, my God, I love you.
And, I will praise you.

I Have Not Trusted

When the weight of all my fears, crush down on me,
Every doubt, every concern, every worry,
Every thought that lacks faith,

So heavy—that I can't move,
So heavy—that I can't breath,
So heavy—that life is a burden,

I turn to you;
I call to you;
I cry out to you.

Rescue me, my Lord.
I have not trusted you, as my provider. I repent.
For only you have provide for me. All is your provision.
Even each breath I take, is your creation.
Every day I have is but your gift.

Rescue me, my God.
I have not trusted you, as my protector. I repent.
For only you protect me. Your might stands alone.
Who can hope to take, what your hand holds
That your great wings protect.

Rescue me, my Father.
I have not trusted you, to know me. I repent.
For only you truly know me. You knew me before I took my first breath.
I was created by your hand, for you.
It is your plan that I know you, and serve you.

Rescue me, my dear Jesus.
I have not trusted you, to love me. I repent.
For only you have died for me, taking my debt upon yourself,
Rescuing me from death, opening the gates of heaven before me
Leading me home.

My God,
I must trust in you.
You have proved yourself worthy.

My Praise

This is my praise for you, Lord.
In everyway and in everything you are with me.
You have never left me, and you have set me on the right path, after each fall.
You have healed me, strengthened me. You have opened my mind, given me knowledge of you.
How—am I not blessed?

This is my heart crying out, in the day of sorrow,
For you are my comfort, Lord.
Your fingers catch my every tear, and your palm holds them.
The pool of my sorrows are in your hand, and you know and are the answer for them all.
How—am I not loved?

This is my heart singing out in joy, in love,
For the peace you have given me, Lord.
Your spirit rests upon me, giving me rest from the burdens of this life:
Blessed relief in the day of trouble, calm in the storm, the light of life in the face of death
How—am I not protected?

This is my heart beating proudly, in awe,
For you are my God and your power is evident, Lord.
Your handiwork shows in the smallest thing to the greatest.
Your mark is upon the atom. Your mark is upon man. Your mark is upon all that is the universe.
How—can I not praise you?

I will praise you.
You alone! You alone!
My God, my Savior, my healer, my comforter, my protector, my creator
This is my praise for you—my Lord.

Some Ask

Some ask:
What has God done for me?
What would God do for me?
What price would God pay for me?
What would God give for me?

I know my price was dear, costly indeed.
God, the Father, held nothing back.

He gave that which is most dear.
He laid down, his only begotten son, on the alter;
My Lord Jesus.
He died, in my stead, on that cross: that wretched tree.

His blood, his life given, that I might have life—everlasting.
Thank you, Father, my God.
Thank you, my Lord, Jesus.

It Is Finished

My Lord Jesus, my savior, My King,
I would not take one lash from your body.
How then could I be healed?

I would not have prevented you from going, to the cross.
I would not have taken your place, at the cross.
I would not have let you down, from the cross,
Till you had breathed your last.

For if I did
My sin would still be upon me,
My only hope lost,
Separated from you and the Father forever.

My Lord Jesus, I am so sorry that my life came at such a cost.
It was your love—for me.
It was your love—for the world.
So, that we could share in your life
That you took back, after three days
And, have a place in the kingdom of Heaven.

Only your life could,
Only your life can
Cover—my stains;
Cover—the stains of the world.

You alone—are worthy.
You alone—could stand before the Father,
And proclaim, "It is finished."

Soaring

When the prince of the air beats against us,
When the storms of the world,
When the storms of Satan are all about us
We will rise like eagles on the never failing wings of the Word.

Riding the currents,
Soaring above the tempest, or with the Lord's strength,
Wings beating struggling against the wind, the rain, and the hail: all the storm's fury
We will pass through the storm.
Resisting Satan till the storm is past, till he has fled.

Knowing the Father has his great wings about us
And, his son, the Lord Jesus, leads the way;
The Spirit within giving us comfort.
We will not be beaten.
The victory is the Lords.

No Friend Like You

Lord Jesus,
There is no friend like you.
I will always use your name.
What man has a friend that he does not call him by name?
As you have said, "No one has greater love than this: to lay his life down
for his friends."
(John 15:13MLB)
You have laid your life down for me, for the world.
You have traded your perfect pure life in exchange for my sinful corrupt
life,
For the lives of all who come to know you.
You are my greatest friend.
Jesus! Jesus! Jesus!
Who, is like you?

Though, the world does not now you. You are its greatest friend
Saving any, who believe on you.
Open their eyes, open their ears, and open their hearts, Lord.
Increase the harvest
So, that more can know you and proclaim,
"Jesus! Jesus! Jesus!
Who, is like you?"

What friend, removes your every debt?
What friend, removes you every hurt?
Only you, Lord.
You have paid in full, for all.

Who else, has sent the Holy Spirit to bring us joy in our trials?
Who else, has opened the gates of heaven: to eternal life?
Only you Lord.
All is given into your hands.

What a friend you are.
What a friend you are.
I will use your name,
Jesus, my Lord—Jesus.

Once Again

Oh my Lord—Jesus, cleanse me once again
With your holy life, your holy blood.
Cover, once again, my sin and my weakness
With your perfect life, and your great strength.
Once again, make me pure before the Father.

Oh my Lord, once again, I have been a fool.
Once again, I have set my eyes to worldly things.
Once again, I have set my mind to the longings, to the imaginings
common to man.
Once again, I have set my heart to the desires, to the lusts of the flesh.

Oh my Lord, once again, and again and again I am the fool.
Once again, I fail you.
Once again, I turn from you.
Once again, I am wretched.

Oh my Lord, once again, my accuser is upon me.
Once again, I am assailed by the cost of my sin.
Once again, I am condemned in my heart.
Once again, the enemy gloats over me, before you.

Oh my Lord, once again, you convict me.
Once again, you call me out of my sin.
Once again, I look to you; I bow down.
Once again, I confess and repent.

Oh my Lord, once again, in all your patience,
Once again, as you show your love to me,
Once again, as you shape me to your will,
Once again, till I am the fool no longer.

Oh my Lord, Jesus, cleanse me once again
With your holy life, your holy blood
Cover, once again, my sin and my weakness
With your perfect life, and your great strength.
Once again, make me pure before the Father.

My Lord Saw Me

My Lord saw me.
He saw me—lost and alone.
He saw me—in debt and penniless.
He saw me—set upon and defenseless.
He saw me—dead in my sin,
Bound for hell, separated from the Father's love.

He saw me—and he loved me.
He saw me—and forgave me.
He saw me—and came for me.
He saw me—and died for me.

My Lord saw me—and came for me.
Now I am found, and he is always with me.
My Lord saw me—and paid for me.
Now I am free, and in his blessings.
My Lord saw me—and saved me from my enemies.
Now I am alive, and bound for heaven: my Father's house.

My lord saw me.
He saw me—in all my stains.
He saw me—in all my wickedness.
He saw me—in all my pride.
He saw me—in all my selfishness.

He saw me—and he loved me.
He saw me—and forgave me.
He saw me—and came for me.
He saw me—and died for me.

My Lord saw me—and washed away all my sins, my stains,
And made me clean.
My Lord saw me—and took away my wickedness,
And gave me his love.
My Lord saw me—and crushed my pride,
And showed me his might: his power.
My Lord saw me—and took my selfish heart,
And gave me a heart for others: a heart like his.

My Lord saw me.
He sees me.
His eyes are always on me.
My Lord—he is always with me.

In the Rough

God finds us in the rough.
In appearance—as any other common stone,
Highly flawed, plain,
Worthless, in the eyes of the world;
Precious, to the Father.

God sees to our hearts,
To the jewel of faith within.
We are searched for, and taken from the many.
Set apart to be worked
To reveal, what the Father sees in us.

God, through trials, shapes us.
Every flaw is removed.
Each crack and pit is cut away.
Each facet is ground and polished,
Taking in and reflecting the light

We are God's treasure,
Each of us, a work of his hand.
First created, then shaped into his perfect will.
Each gem being worked into a jewel, highly prized of the Father.
Each jewel placed, shines for his purpose.

Transform Me

Put your hand upon me, Lord.
Set to working on your temple.
Make it strong, so that it will not fall.
Till it is, the temple you desire,
A dwelling place of your Holy Spirit.

Guide me, Lord; lead me.
Set me, on the path you have for me.
Turn me, from each false way.
Till I follow after your voice only,
A lamb of your flock.

Rest your Spirit upon me, Lord.
Bathe me in his flames.
Burn from me every flaw.
Till I am the vessel you want for your use,
A servant fully in your will.

Fashion me, Lord, to your will.
Make of me that which pleases you.
Make of me all that you would have me be.
A child of the Father
Loved, adored, cherished; worth any cost.

In all things, Lord, set me to your will.
So, that I will be as pleasing to you, as I am loved.

A Servant Before You

I have not been before you, as I should.
I have stood before your throne
With a halting heart,
With a double mind: doubting.

A servant unable to serve,
Untrained,
Lacking in ability, and understanding;
Useless to the Lord, and the Kingdom.

It is in my heart, to be before you, as I should.
To stand before your throne,
Not only
With all my heart,
With all my mind.

But,
With a steadfast heart,
With a single mind: believing.

A servant who serves well,
Trained,
Fully capable, and who knows his duties;
Used of the Lord, an asset to the Kingdom.

Whose heart is to perform your will,
Who looks to you, in all things,
Seeking you in your word, and in prayer,
A man after your heart.

Lord, I am looking, to you
Lord, I am waiting, on you
Lord, I am following, after you
Lord, I am, your servant

The Path

Lord Jesus, my shining savior,
Blessed light of the world
The hope of the world is in you.
You are a beacon to the lost.
An overwhelming brilliance

That burns away
All darkness,
Every shadow,
Every hidden thing.

The snares,
The traps,
And the pitfalls
Of each false path are made plain.

The path is clear in your light, oh Lord.
The one true path is revealed.

Through the light of your word,
You show the way.

The way has been made clear,
By your sacrifice at the cross.

You are seated on your throne.
Shining in your glory.
Arms open wide to all,
Who look to your light.

Following the narrow path
That leads to you,
That leads to the life you promise:
Life everlasting.

Covering

The vileness of my sins, that were upon my life,
Were put upon him: my stains.
My death was his covering, on that cross.

The Father looked from him, forsaking him,
As my sin was laid upon him.
Clothed in my stains he descended into hell,
In my place, on that day.

The purity of his uprightness before God, that was upon his life,
Has been put upon me: his righteousness.
His life is my covering, before the Father.

The Father looks upon me, accepting me,
For I am covered in his life, his blood.
Clothed in his righteousness I am welcomed into heaven,
In his name, on this day.

I Rely on You

I rely, on your grace and your mercy
And every promise of your word.
I place my life in your strong hands.
My family and all those I love,
I give into your loving embrace.

Your wings of protection are unfailing.
In you, I can be sure.
I trust in you, Lord Jesus, my God.
All that matters to me, I give to you.

Over All

My Father,
My God,
You are so powerful—so mighty,
Beyond my ability to know.

But, this I do know.
All my weaknesses are nothing before you
Every evil plan of Hell,
Each flesh driven thought,
My every sin,
My every illness,
My every hurt;
My every lack.

You are over them all.
They have no power, over your will.
They have no voice, before your word.
They are barely mist, before your presence.

A touch of your hand,
A word from your mouth,
And they are gone
Like they never were.

Father—you are over these.
Yet, not these only,
You are master over all:
The one true God.
You alone rule.

My Father,
As you look upon me,
As I pass through this life,
In the times of plenty: of ease,
In the times of lack: of need,

Be with me always.
Keep my faith in you
My eyes, my heart, my mind on you
That you will rule over my every day
That you will see me through.

I know—on you, I can be sure.
For you, Father—are my help, my comfort, my God.
As is your will
Through, my Lord Jesus.

Questions

Oh Lord, questions, so many questions
Are asked in disbelief.
Our understanding flawed
What of death? What of pain?
What of war? What of hunger?
What of disease? What of lies?
What of hate? What of every evil?

Oh Lord, as our belief grows,
As our understanding is refined,
Will we come to say?
If there were no death,
Would life be so precious?
If there were no pain,
Would pleasure be so sweet?
If there were no war,
Would peace be so pursued?
If there were no hunger,
Would food have such savor?
If there were no disease,
Would health be so prized?
If there were no lies,
Would truth be so rare?
If there were no hate,
Would love be so longed for?
If there were no evil cursed things,
Would any blessing be known, for its worth?

Oh Lord, we are so blind.
In this world it is only thorough the curses
That the blessings are made plain
That their worth is known.

So Lord, we praise you
For both the blessings and the curses.

For through them we know
The blessings of serving Heaven,
Of serving you Lord, our God.
For through them we know
The curses of serving the World,
Of serving the flesh.

Life and death are before us.
The choice is ours.
We choose life.
We choose you, Lord.

Your Enemy, Your Friend

How I hate, that I was your enemy.
That I chose, to side with the world
Hells close ally.
That I looked at death, and found it lovely:
Something, to be desired;
Something, to be pursued;
Desiring to partake of the poison
That this world, calls life.

How I hate, that I did not know
Good from evil.
That I have, in my ignorance,
Given worldly advice.
Believing, I had done well.
Believing, I had done good.
Well pleased, in sowing the seeds of death.

How I hate, that being loved of the world
Mattered to me.
To be thought of, as one of the many.
That I desired to have men speak well of me.
My words and my deeds
Were like those of the world:
As worldly minded, as any of the unsaved;
Wanting to be, as one of the dead.

Oh my God, in these ways and more,
I have been against you.
I have not respected your gift, my salvation:
I have treated it roughly,
I have abused it,
I have neglected it,
I have not held it to its high value.

Where, I have been unfaithful.
You have been patient.
You have seen me through trials.
You have chastened me.
You have brought me to understanding.
You have been faithful.
You have been my loving Father.

How I love that, I am now your friend.
That I have chosen to side with Heaven.
That I am the Lord's ally.
That I look to life, and know it to be lovely.
This is to be desired.
This is to be pursued.
To partake of the Word: this is food, food indeed;
This is life, life indeed.

How I love, that I now know
Good from evil,
Revealed through the Word.
Your Word is truth.
Speaking it,
I know I have done well.
I know I have done good.
I am well satisfied in sowing the seeds of life

How I love, that I am loved in heaven,
This is all that matters
To be among the few who are called,
Chosen out of the world, by the Father.
My words and my deeds
Are those of the saved.
I rejoice in being among those that live.

Oh my God, how I am turned to you.
How, I am for you.
How glad I am in your gift, my salvation:
Now I treat it tenderly.
Now I feed it.
Now I care for it.
Now I know its worth, its high value.

In Your Hands

Father, Thank you
For keeping me in your hands,
For not putting me aside,
For continuing to work on me,
Forming me—shaping me to your will.

Taking from me my flaws,
Adding to me your perfection,
As you make me more and more
Like my Lord, who is Jesus.

Thank You

Father, thank you for those
Who teach and speak your Word,
Who instruct us in your Word,
To help us to know you;
Pastors, faithful to you and your Word.

Father, thank you for those
Who write and sing your praises,
Who share with us their love for you,
To help us to raise our voices in praise of you;
Worship leaders, rejoicing in you and your Word.

Father, thank you for those
Who everyday are a help to us,
Who do the work that is not seen,
To help us to be focused on you;
Servants, preparing the way for you and your Word.

Father, thank you for those
Who are filled with the Holy Spirit,
Expressing the gifts of the Spirit,
Who show your power, through your servants,
Who share your words,
That you would speak to us now,
To help us to see your power, and to be in awe of it;
Servants, acting in your will, according to your Word.

Father, thank you for your miracles
That you work in each of our lives.
Showing personally your love for each of us,
To help us as only you can,
When we most need it,
Our God, the Most High God;
Showing his will in our lives.

Father, thank you for all you do for us.
For our Lord Jesus sake.

Your Will

Not what I want,
Not when I want it,
Not how I want it, Lord.

But, in all things, let it be
What you want,
When you want it,
How you want it, Lord.

The blessing I want,
Is not the best for me.
The moment I want your blessing,
Is not the best time to have that blessing.
The way I want to receive your blessing,
Is not how I should receive that blessing, Lord.

You know what I need,
The blessings that are best for me
That lead me closer to you.

You know when I have need,
When the time is right for me to receive your blessings,
When I'll be drawn closer to you.

You know the way
That best leads to the blessings you have for me,
The way that leads me closer to you.

So Lord, in all ways, be over me.
So Lord, not my will, but yours.

God's Love

This—is his love sent.
This—is God's song.
This—is God's gift.
This—is God's will toward men.

On the day that his only begotten son was born,
His angel rang out this message,
Along with the host of heaven,
"Glory to God in the highest, and on earth peace, good will toward men."
(Luke 2:14 NKJV)
Our savior born into the world,
Our Lord, Jesus;
The Word made flesh.

He came—to live among us.
He came—to teach us.
He came—to die for us, that we might live.
He came—to show us the depth of God's love, for us.

The meaning of,
"Glory to God in the highest, and on earth peace, good will toward men."
(Luke 2:14 NKJV)
That we are loved indeed.
That we are cherished indeed.
That God would hold nothing back from us.
That God would give anything for us.

Rejoice in God—for his gift to us.
Rejoice in Jesus—our savior.
Rejoice in the Holy Spirit—who is sent to us.

Great and Wonderful God

What a great and wonderful God,
We have.

He helps the great and the small,
The wealthy and the poor,
The leaders and the workers,
Those who rule nations,
And those who have nothing.

None are respected of God.
All are loved of God.
For those who reach out to him in faith,
Our God is strong and mighty.
He meets every need.

What a great and wonderful God,
We have.

To Serve and Follow

Father, as my Lord Jesus served you,
I want to serve you.
As he lead the way,
I want to follow.

I want to follow after the ways of life,
Not to follow after the ways of death.

I want to do those things:
That are of the spirit,
That are of life,
That are of Heaven,
That are of you—my God.

I do not want to do, those things
That are of the flesh,
That are of death,
That are of Hell,
That are of our enemy—Satan.

Father, as my Lord Jesus served you,
I want to serve you,
As he lead the way,
I want to follow.

When I Look

When I look at what I have suffered,
What I thought was suffering.
Then I look at what you have suffered,
At the suffering you knew.

How little I knew of suffering, my Lord

When I look at how I faced what I have suffered,
What I thought was strong.
Then I look at how you faced your suffering;
At the strength shown, in your forgiveness, at the cross.

How little I knew of strength, my Lord.

Lord, you have suffered above all.
Lord, you are strong above all.
Lord, I am in awe of you.

Your Love for Me

In every way, I have fallen short.
In my every sinful thought,
In every sinful thing I've done,
You have hated my sin
But, never me.

You have always loved me.
You have longed after me
First to come to you,
Then to return to you
After each fall.

And, I know that if I had never come to know you
And, was cast into Hell.
Still, you would have loved me.
It would have been I, who hated you.
It would have been I, who chose my separation from you.
Refusing to see you, as the Lord, you are:
Lord over all.

Up to the moment of my judgment,
You would have called me to repentance:
Into your loving embrace,
Forgiven of all,
To be as I am now.

Father, thank you for my Lord—Jesus.
For through him and by him,
I thank you for my salvation.

My Strength

You are my strength, to continue,
When there is no clear path.
You are my strength, to remain,
When all have left my side.
You are my strength, to stand,
When all my strength has left me.
You are my strength, to overcome,
When all seems lost.

No matter—the foe,
No matter—my weakness,
No matter—if any stand with me,
No matter—my path;
No matter—any adversity

I will not fear.
You are with me, Lord.
You are my strength.
I will call on you,
And you—will see me through.

Amen

Printed in the United States
86076LV00005B/661-684/A